The OFFICIAL ENGLAND Annual 2012

Written by Jon Culley

Designed by Brian Thomson

A Grange Publication

Published by Grange Communications Ltd., Edinburgh, under licence from The Football Association Ltd. Printed in the EU.

ISBN: 978-1-908221-41-4

£7.99

Contents

Managers

1946 - 1974

England's first international match was against Scotland in 1872 but there was no England manager until Walter Winterbottom in 1946. Previously, it had been down to a selection committee to pick coaches and trainers as well as the players.

Winterbottom still did not pick the team but under his guidance England reached the World Cup Finals four times in a row from 1950 to 1962. He also laid down new national coaching standards and set up Youth and Under-23 England teams.

Alf Ramsey, who took over in 1963, was the first England manager to have full control over selection, training and tactics. A pioneer of the 4-4-2 system, Ramsey had his critics but England's 1966 World Cup triumph silenced his doubters.

Ramsey's team was third in the 1968 European Championship but his stock fell when England lost to West Germany from 2-0 up in the quarter-finals in the 1970 World Cup and he was dismissed after failing to qualify for the 1974 Finals.

Sir Walter **Winterbottom**

Born: Oldham. 31 January, 1913.

Centre-half for Manchester United from 1936-38. Retired through injury aged 25.

Appointed FA's director of coaching and England team manager in 1946.

Led England to Finals of 1950, 1954, 1958 and 1962 World Cups. Best finish: Quarter-finalists (1954 & 1962).

Resigned after 1962 World Cup.

England record: P 139 W 78 D 33 L 28

Knighted: 1978.

Died: 16 February, 2002, aged 89.

Sir Alf **Ramsey**

Born: Dagenham, 22 January, 1920.

Right-back for Southampton and Tottenham Hotspur. Earned 32 England caps from 1948-53 and scored 3 goals, all penalties.

Won the First Division title as a player with Tottenham.

As a manager, he took Ipswich Town from Third Division (South) in 1955 to the First Division title by 1962.

Appointed England manager in 1963, predicting England would win the World Cup.

Fulfilled his promise when England won the 1966 World Cup, beating West Germany 4-2 after extra time in the Wembley Final.

Lost to Yugoslavia in the semi-finals of the European Championship in Italy in 1968.

Reached quarter-finals of the 1970 World Cup in Mexico, where England lost 3-2 to West Germany after leading 2-0.

Failed to qualify for the 1974 World Cup Finals after inspired Polish goalkeeper Jan Tomaszewski denied them at Wembley.

Sacked in May 1974, returning later to club football, retiring in 1980.

England record: P 113 W 69 D 27 L 17

Knighted: 1967.

Died: 28 April, 1999, aged 79.

1974 - 1982

After Ramsey, England turned to Joe Mercer, who had won every domestic honour as Manchester City manager. But Mercer, by then Coventry City boss, was hired only as a stop-gap for seven matches, and in July 1974 the equally successful Leeds manager, Don Revie, was installed.

As a player, Revie was famed as a master tactician, as a manager for his detailed 'dossiers' on opposing teams. But England failed to qualify for the 1976 European Championship and defeat to Italy in Rome in October 1976 made it unlikely they would reach the 1978 World Cup Finals in Argentina.

Revie resigned amid controversy in July 1977, taking a highly-paid job in the Middle East, and England's next choice was Ron Greenwood, who had been West Ham's manager for 13 years and previously worked with England's Youth and Under-23 teams.

The highly-respected Greenwood took England to the 1980 European Championship Finals and the 1982 World Cup, where they were unlucky to be eliminated without losing a match. He stepped down soon afterwards.

Joe **Mercer**

Born: Ellesmere Port, 9 August, 1914.

A left-sided defensive wing-half for Everton, Mercer played five times for England.

As a manager he won the League Cup with Aston Villa before his partnership with coach Malcolm Allison brought the Championship, The FA Cup, the League Cup and the European Cup Winners' Cup to Manchester City.

England record: P 7 W 3 D 3 L 1

Died: 9 August, 1990.

Don **Revie**

Born: Middlesbrough, 10 July, 1927.

Revie played as a forward for five clubs between 1944 and 1962 and won 6 England caps.

As Leeds manager, Revie won two League championships, the League and FA Cups and twice won the Inter-Cities' Fairs Cup.

England were unbeaten in Revie's first season but failed to qualify for the 1976 European Championship Finals and looked unlikely to qualify for the 1978 World Cup Finals in Argentina when he quit to be coach of United Arab Emirates.

England record: P 29 W 14 D 8 L 7

Died: 26 May, 1989.

Ron **Greenwood**

Born: Worsthorne, nr Burnley, 11 November, 1921.

A centre-half, Greenwood never played for England but won the League title with Chelsea.

Coached England's Youth and Under-23s and won The FA Cup and the European Cup Winners' Cup during 13 years as West Ham manager.

Under Greenwood, England qualified for the 1980 European Championship and the 1982 World Cup in Spain, where they did not lose a game but went out after two draws in the second group phase. Greenwood resigned in the aftermath.

England record: P 55 W 33 D 12 L10

Died: 9 February, 2006.

1982-1994

The press clamoured for Brian Clough but England turned next to Bobby Robson, who had enjoyed success with Ipswich Town. Robson had a turbulent time initially and offered to resign when a home defeat to Denmark cost them a place in the 1984 European Championship Finals.

But his offer was turned down and he went on to become England's most successful manager after Ramsey, at least in terms of World Cup performances. A quarter-final in Mexico in 1986, where England were beaten by Argentina in the match infamous for Diego Maradona's 'Hand of God' goal, was followed by a semi-final in Italia '90, where West Germany beat England on penalties.

Robson left after the 1990 Finals and became highly successful in Europe with PSV Eindhoven, Porto and Barcelona.

Graham Taylor, the former Watford manager who had revived Aston Villa, was next in the England hot seat but lasted little more than three years, his reign marked by a poor performance at the Finals of the 1992 European Championship and savage treatment by the media, and a failure to qualify for the 1994 World Cup.

Bobby **Robson**

Born: Sacriston, Co. Durham. 18 February, 1933.

An inside-forward with Fulham and West Brom, he won 20 England caps, scoring 4 goals.

As a manager, he established Ipswich Town as a top-six team in the First Division and won The FA Cup and the UEFA Cup.

Lost only once in 28 qualification matches as England manager but that one defeat cost him a place at the 1984 European Championship.

Led England to the quarter-finals of the 1986 World Cup and a controversial defeat to Diego Maradona's Argentina.

Robson's fortunes dipped when England lost all three group games at the 1988 European Finals but rose again at Italia '90 when his team, group winners, beat Belgium and Cameroon to face West Germany for a place in the Final, only to suffer the heartbreak of defeat on penalties.

After England, Robson won the Dutch and Portuguese titles with PSV Eindhoven and Porto, plus the Spanish Cup and European Cup-Winners' Cup with Barcelona before finishing his career with Newcastle.

England record: P 95 W 47 D 30 L 18

Knighted: 2002.

Died: 31 July, 2009.

Graham **Taylor**

Born: Worksop, Notts. 15 September, 1944.

A full-back with Grimsby and Lincoln, Taylor won the Fourth Division title with Lincoln as manager before leading Watford from the Fourth to the First Division in only five years before taking charge of Aston Villa.

England lost only once in Taylor's first 23 matches as manager but were knocked out of the 1992 European Championship by Sweden. Resigned after failing to qualify for the 1994 World Cup Finals in the USA.

Returned to club management, taking Watford into the top flight for a second time, before retiring in 2003.

England record: P 38 W 18 D 13 L 7

1994-2000

A turbulent six years began when Terry Venables took over from Taylor as the perfect candidate in football terms but with uncertainty surrounding his business affairs.

Venables had won the Spanish League title as manager of Barcelona and reached the Final of the European Cup. England were hosts for Euro '96 and played superbly at times, beating the Netherlands 4-1 before falling to Germany in the semi-finals, again on penalties.

Venables stepped down, but the choice of Glenn Hoddle as his successor promised more of the same and England were among the favourites for the France '98 World Cup.

But they went out in the second round -- again on penalties -- and when Hoddle, in a newspaper interview, made some ill-judged comments about people with disabilities, he was sacked.

Kevin Keegan took over from Hoddle but stayed for only 18 matches. England qualified for Euro 2000 but did not progress beyond the group stage and after losing at home to Germany in the first qualification game for the 2002 World Cup -- the last game at the old Wembley -- Keegan resigned.

Terry Venables

Born: Dagenham, 6 January, 1943.

Venables played in midfield for Chelsea, Tottenham, QPR and Crystal Palace, winning 2 England caps.

As a manager, he took Palace into the First Division and QPR to their first FA Cup Final before going to Spain, where he secured Barcelona's first La Liga title for 11 years.

Back in England as Tottenham manager, he won The FA Cup in 1991, tried unsuccessfully to buy the club then became chief executive after businessman Alan Sugar took control, only for the relationship to end in a bitter court battle.

After being England coach, he almost took Australia to the 1998 World Cup, helped Bryan Robson keep Middlesbrough in the Premier League in 2001 and returned to the England bench as Steve McClaren's assistant.

England record: P 23 W 11 D 11 L 1

Glenn Hoddle

Born: Hayes, 27 October, 1957.

A supremely gifted midfield player, Hoddle won The FA Cup twice and the UEFA Cup with Tottenham, plus the French League and Cup with Monaco, as well as 53 England caps.

As a manager with six clubs, however, an FA Cup final with Chelsea was his best achievement.

England record: P 28 W 17 D 6 L 5

Kevin Keegan

Born: Doncaster, 14 February, 1951.

Keegan had a glittering career as a striker with Liverpool, Hamburg, Southampton and Newcastle as well as winning 63 England caps.

Success followed as Newcastle manager, where he won the Division One title and was twice runner-up in the Premier League.

Head-hunted for the England job while at Fulham but resigned after 18 games, claiming he was tactically 'a bit short'.

Returned to club football to win the Division One title again with Manchester City.

England record: P 18 W 7 D 7 L 4

After Keegan, FA technical director Howard Wilkinson took charge of England's second 2002 World Cup qualifier, taking one point against Finland in Helsinki. Peter Taylor supervised a friendly against Italy -- significant for being the first of David Beckham's 58 games as captain.

Then came the appointment of Sven-Goran Eriksson as England's first foreign coach. The Swede, highly successful in club football, won his first five matches, and had a stunning 5-1 victory over Germany in Munich, although it still took a last-gasp equaliser by Beckham against Greece to clinch a place at the 2002 World Cup.

England went out in the quarter-finals, as they did in Euro 2004 and the 2006 World Cup, but by improving England's world ranking from 17th to 5th Eriksson became the most successful England coach after Ramsey.

Eriksson left after the 2006 Finals, after which England sounded out the Brazilian, Luiz Felipe Scolari, before plumping for Eriksson's assistant, Steve McClaren.

Terry Venables returned as McClaren's assistant but England's failure to qualify for Euro 2008 ended with the dismissal of both men.

2000-2007

Sven-Goran Eriksson

Born: Sunne, Sweden, 5 February, 1948.

Eriksson had a modest career as a full-back in Sweden but his achievements as a player were totally eclipsed by his success as a manager.

Before taking the England job, he won 19 trophies, including league and cup doubles in three countries, with Goteborg (Sweden), Benfica (Portugal) and Lazio (Italy).

Took up the job of England coach in January 2001 and -- excluding penalty shoot-outs -- suffered only three defeats in competitive matches in five and a half years in charge.

Under Eriksson, England lost 2-1 to eventual winners Brazil in the quarter-finals at the 2002 World Cup and to Portugal at the same stage of both Euro 2004 and the 2006 World Cup, each time on penalties.

Since stepping down, Eriksson has had spells with the Mexico and Ivory Coast national teams and in club football with Notts County and Leicester City.

England record: P 67 W 40 D 17 L 10

Steve McClaren

Born: York, 3 May, 1961.

A midfield player in lower division football, McClaren worked as a coach at Oxford United and Derby before joining Manchester United as assistant to Sir Alex Ferguson. His first half-season ended with United wining the treble -- Premier League, FA Cup and Champions League -- and they retained the title in 2000 and 2001.

McClaren joined the England coaching staff part-time in 2000 and became manager of Middlesbrough in 2001, winning the Carling Cup and reaching the UEFA Cup final. He succeeded Eriksson as head coach in 2006.

England's qualifying campaign for Euro 2008 under McClaren began with two wins but two points from the next three games set them back and. though they rallied with four wins in a row, defeats in their last two matches cost them a place at the Finals.

McClaren moved on to win the Dutch title with FC Twente and worked with Wolfsburg in Germany before returning to English football with Nottingham Forest.

England record: P 18 W 9 D 4 L 5

SINCE 2007

England looked abroad again for Steve McClaren's successor. Pundits made former Chelsea manager Jose Mourinho the initial favourite but the man who landed the job was Fabio Capello, who had amassed nine league titles in only 16 years as a manager in Italy and Spain.

In five seasons with AC Milan he won four Serie A titles, three Italian Super Cups, the Champions League -- beating Barcelona 4-0 in the final -- and the European Super Cup. He also won the Scudetto with Roma and Juventus (twice), as well as two La Liga titles with Real Madrid.

As a player, Capello starred in midfield for Roma, Juventus and Milan, winning 32 caps for Italy. Capello counts his 1973 goal against England, helping Italy to win at Wembley for the first time, as a highlight of his career.

Capello took England to the 2010 World Cup Finals with a qualifying record of nine wins from 10 matches but his team disappointed in South Africa, losing 4-1 to Germany in the first knock-out round.

Fabio Capello

Born: San Canzian d'Isonzo, Italy, 18 June, 1946.

Capello grew up in a small village not far from Italy's border with Slovenia, playing his first organised football for the local youth team, coached by his father, Guerrino.

His first professional club was SPAL, based in the northern Italian city of Ferrara and then in Serie A.

As a player he won three Italian titles with Juventus and one with AC Milan, as well as the Coppa Italia with Milan and Roma.

He was appointed head coach of AC Milan in 1991 and won the first of his four Serie A titles there a year later.

He coached Real Madrid for one season in 1996-97 and again a decade later, winning La Liga on each occasion.

In between, he guided Roma to their first Scudetto for 18 years and finished top of the table twice with Juventus, although their titles were rescinded later over allegations of match-fixing.

Capello has been married to his wife, Laura, for more than 40 years and they have two children. His son, Pierfilippo, is also his agent.

Away from football, he has travelled extensively, loves opera and has a substantial fine art collection.

GREAT MATCHES #1

England 4, West Germany 2

(after extra time)

Wembley; 30 July, 1966; World Cup Final

Attendance: 96,924.

Goals: Haller (12 min) 0-1; Hurst (18) 1-1; Peters (78) 2-1; Weber (89) 2-2; Hurst (101) 3-2; Hurst (120) 4-2.

Not only was this England's finest hour but one of the most exciting of all World Cup Finals.

Helmut Haller puts the Germans ahead after 12 minutes before Geoff Hurst quickly heads England level. Just 12 minutes from the end, Martin Peters forces England in front.

With a minute left, England think they are home and dry. But then Wolfgang Weber silences a whole nation by poking in an equaliser, ushering in 30 minutes of extra time.

Next, controversy: Hurst crashes a shot against the underside of the bar. It bounces close to the line, but not clearly over. Gottfried Dienst, the Swiss referee, consults Tofik Bakhramov, the linesman from Azerbaijan, and signals a goal.

Its legitimacy remains disputed to this day but England's victory is confirmed in the last minute of extra time when Bobby Moore launches a 40-yard pass into the German half and Hurst gallops away to score his third goal and England's fourth.

ENGLAND 4 GERMANY W. 2

20 QUESTIONS:

05 Which player holds the record for most goals at a World Cup tournament for England?

06 Which central defender scored the last England goal at the old Wembley against Ukraine in May 2000?

01 Which England player scored England's fastest-ever World Cup goal, after just 27 seconds against France in Bilbao in 1982?

02 Which England striker became England's youngest-ever goalscorer, aged 17 years and 317 days, when he netted against Macedonia in 2003?

03 Who became the youngest England player to score a hat-trick, against Croatia in 2008, aged 19 years and 178 days?

04 What happened to David Beckham in Saint-Etienne on 30 June, 1998 and in Manchester on 8 October, 2005?

15

07 What happened to Chris Waddle and Stuart Pearce in Turin on 4 July, 1990?

08 What do George Eastham, Nigel Clough and Frank Lampard have in common?

09 Which Manchester United player represented England schoolboys before winning 64 senior international caps for Wales?

10 Who was England's manager when the Sun newspaper reported a European Championship defeat under the headline "Swedes 2 Turnips 1"?

11 Which Northumberland-born defender captained his club to three Premier League titles in the 1990s but was never picked for his country?

12 Which England manager made David Beckham captain for the first time?

13 Who used to be known as the 'best manager England never had'.

14 What do Ron Greenwood, Graham Taylor and Steve McClaren have in common?

15 Which Tottenham striker scored six times for England as a substitute between October 2008 and September 2009?

16 What was special about defender Viv Anderson's England debut against Czechoslovakia in November 1978?

17 Who became England's tallest player when he made his debut against United States in May 2005 but lost the distinction when Peter Crouch was selected against Colombia three days later?

18 What happened to England in Belo Horizonte on 29 June, 1950?

19 Which midfielder in England's Italia 90 squad played for three different Italian clubs during his England career?

20 Which England player won 50 of his 115 caps while playing for clubs outside England?

Answers on Page 60

V
SWITZERLAND
2011

Goalkeepers

Joe Hart

Born 19 April, 1987

Joe Hart has experienced a meteoric rise to become a top choice in the England goal, and there is every reason to believe the 6ft 3ins Manchester City 'keeper will hold the position for some time to come.

After beginning his career with home-town club Shrewsbury Town, Hart moved to City in 2006, where he would become Sven-Goran Eriksson's first-choice 'keeper within a year. However, after the arrival of Shay Given in January 2009, he spent the 2009-10 season on loan at Birmingham City.

A series of heroic displays at St Andrews, helping Birmingham to their highest ever Premier League finish, raised his stock again and he returned to Eastlands in 2010 to reclaim the number one spot. He won the Barclays Golden Glove award in 2010-11 for the most Premier League clean sheets in helping City qualify for the Champions League.

After first excelling for England's Under-21s, saving and scoring a penalty in the semi-final shoot-out win over Sweden at Euro 2009, Hart has seamlessly made the transition to the senior side. He made his debut in 2008 against Trinidad & Tobago, and has become a regular since the 2010 World Cup.

Joe Hart

DID YOU KNOW?

Joe could have been a professional cricketer and spent two years at the Worcestershire Academy before choosing a career in football.

Scott **Carson**

Born 3 September, 1985

After a frustrating start to his senior club career, Scott Carson realised his potential after a move to West Bromwich Albion in 2008 gave him a regular first-team role.

After beginning his professional career at Leeds United, the 6ft 'keeper completed a high-profile move to Liverpool in 2005 following the Yorkshire club's relegation from the Premier League.

Despite showing promise and frequently being labelled as a 'future England number one', he largely played second fiddle to Jerzy Dudek at Anfield and only in loan spells at Charlton in 2006 and Aston Villa in 2007 did he play regularly.

It came as no surprise when Carson left Merseyside for newly-promoted West Brom in 2008. He was unable to save the club from relegation from the Premier League in 2009 but captained the club to promotion from the Championship in 2010.

An agile 'keeper often praised for his shot-stopping ability, Whitehaven-born Carson made a record 29 Under-21 appearances and was given his full England debut against Austria in 2007. Now with Bursaspor in the Turkish Super Lig, the goalkeeper will be ready when his country calls again.

DID YOU KNOW?

Scott's younger brother Grant was on Crewe and Carlisle's books as a 'keeper but now plays as a striker in the Cumberland League.

Robert **Green**

Born 18 January, 1980

Robert Green has been a consistent goalkeeper in the Premier League but has had to wait patiently for opportunities on the international stage.

He became the sixth Norwich City player to be capped for England at senior level when he made his debut as substitute for James in the friendly against Colombia in New Jersey in May 2005.

But the form of Paul Robinson and David James meant Surrey-born Green had to wait four years for his first start, in the 2010 World Cup qualifier against Kazakhstan in June 2009. He went to the 2010 World Cup Finals, where he appeared in England's opening match with the USA. He had missed the 2006 Finals through injury.

After helping Norwich win promotion to the Premier League, 6ft 3ins Green signed for West Ham United in August 2006 and was voted 'Hammer of the Year' in 2008.

He was unable to stave off West Ham's relegation to the Championship in 2011, but won frequent praise for excelling in a struggling team.

Renowned for his record in saving penalties, Green has the less enviable distinction of being the only England goalkeeper ever to be sent off in an international match.

DID YOU KNOW?

Robert climbed Mount Kilimanjaro in Tanzania during a charity event for the African Medical and Research Foundation (AMREF).

Goalkeeping Greats:

Gordon Banks

1963-72; Caps: 73.

Gordon Banks will forever remain part of England's football folklore as one of our 1966 World Cup heroes but would be seen as one of the finest goalkeepers of his or any other era regardless of his role in England's victory over West Germany in the Wembley Final.

He was still England's number one in the Mexico World Cup four years later and underlined his reputation when he spectacularly kept out Pelé's header in the game against Brazil in Guadalajara, a stunning piece of athleticism that became known as the 'Save of the Century'.

Capped 73 times by his country, he would surely have extended his career but for a car crash in 1972 that cost him his sight in one eye and forced him to quit prematurely at the age of 34.

Born in Sheffield in 1937, Banks began his career with Chesterfield. His progress was interrupted by national service but once he had made his debut in November 1958 his talent was quickly spotted and he was signed by First Division Leicester City after only 23 appearances.

He stayed at Leicester for eight years before spending five seasons with Stoke. He was awarded an OBE in 1970.

Gordon Banks

Peter Shilton

1970-90; Caps: 125.

Peter Shilton played almost 1,400 games for 11 clubs during a professional career that spanned close to 31 years. Having made his debut for home town club Leicester City in May 1966 -- aged just 16 -- he finally called it a day in January 1997, when he made his 1005th League appearance at the age of 47, for Leyton Orient. He remains England's most-capped player, with 125 appearances in a 20-year career and would have made more had he not had such fierce competition from Ray Clemence, with whom he alternated in the England goal during the 1970s and '80s.

A brilliant shot-stopper, Shilton made his England debut for Sir Alf Ramsey against East Germany in November 1970. With Shilton in goal, England won 66 times and conceded only 80 goals. He kept a record 65 clean sheets.

He bowed out on a high at Italia '90, having helped England achieve their best World Cup performance since 1966 by reaching the semi-finals. Shilton's last game in an England shirt was the third-place play-off against hosts Italy.

Shilton's domestic career reached a peak with Nottingham Forest, where he won the First Division Championship, the League Cup and the European Cup twice. He has been awarded an OBE and MBE for services to football.

Peter Shilton

European Championships Tournament History

1960, Lev Yashin

1960: France, Winners: Soviet Union

UEFA launched the first European Nations' Cup in 1960. It was won by the Soviet Union, captained by legendary goalkeeper Lev Yashin, who beat Yugoslavia 2-1 in the Final in Paris thanks to a goal in extra time.

Only 17 teams entered, with England, Italy and West Germany staying away, and games were played as a home-and-away knock-out to produce four finalists. Spain pulled out for political reasons after being drawn to meet the Soviets in the last eight, denying the stars of five-times European club champions Real Madrid the chance to shine on the international stage.

After reaching the last four, France were chosen to host the Semi-Finals and Final but their dreams of reaching the first Final were dashed when they lost 5-4 to Yugoslavia, despite leading 4-2 with only 15 minutes left.

1964: Spain, Winners: Spain

The entry increased to 29 for the second Championship, with all British home nations apart from Scotland persuaded to take part. Again the competition followed a knock-out format until the semi-finals. England were only two years away from their 1966 World Cup triumph but did not survive the preliminary round, losing 6-3 on aggregate to France.

Spain hosted the Semi-Final and Final rounds and after beating Hungary 2-1 after extra time their opponents in the Final were the Soviet Union, whom they had refused to play four years earlier over Soviet support for the socialist Republicans in the Spanish Civil War.

This time, dictator General Franco agreed to let them play and -- much to his pleasure -- the Spaniards won 2-1 with [illegible] and Marcelino Martínez.

1968: Italy, Winners: Italy

Qualifying groups were introduced for the first time, with the eight group winners meeting in the quarter-finals over two legs. The Home Internationals of 1966-67 and 1968-69 served as one group. England, by then World champions, pipped Scotland by one point despite losing 3-2 at home to the Auld Enemy.

England beat Spain 3-1 on aggregate in their quarter-final but lost a bruising semi-final with Yugoslavia in Florence by the only goal after Alan Mullery became the first England player to be sent off in a full international.

Italy won the tournament. Their semi-final against the Soviet Union was decided on the toss of a coin after a 120-minute stalemate, and they won the final in a replay, beating Yugoslavia 2-0 with goals from Luigi Riva and Pietro Anastasi.

1972: Belgium, Winners: West Germany

West Germany confirmed their position as the new force in Europe by winning the 1972 Championship.

England had dropped only one point to qualify from a group containing Greece, Switzerland and Malta but were outclassed by Franz Beckenbauer and company in the first leg of their quarter-final, at Wembley.

West Germany, building for the 1974 World Cup, won 3-1 and England could only salvage a 0-0 draw in the second leg in Berlin. The Germans grew stronger. In the finals, held in Belgium, they beat the hosts 2-1 and demolished the Soviet Union in the final, winning 3-0. Gerd Müller, scourge of England in the Mexico World Cup, scored twice in each match.

1968, Alan Mullery

1976: Yugoslavia, Winners: Czechoslovakia

Under new manager Don Revie, England's qualifying campaign began with a resounding 3-0 win over Czechoslovakia at Wembley. But a goalless draw at home to Portugal became costly when Czechoslovakia recovered from Mick Channon's early goal to beat England in Bratislava, after which a 1-1 draw against Portugal in Lisbon was not enough.

Czechoslovakia went on to be crowned champions at the Finals in Yugoslavia, which featured four outstanding games that all went to extra time but also produced 19 goals.

The counter-attacking Czechs overcame the 'total football' of the Netherlands 3-1 in the first semi-final; then West Germany came from behind to beat the hosts 4-2. The Dutch scored in extra time to win the third-place match 3-2 and the resilient Germans recovered from 2-0 down to 2-2 in the Final, only to lose in a penalty shoot-out.

1976, Mick Channon

1980: Italy, Winners: West Germany

Under Ron Greenwood, England qualified comfortably from a group including Northern Ireland and the Republic of Ireland, Denmark and Bulgaria. They were held 1-1 in Dublin in their second game but after that won six in a row.

There were eight finalists for the first time, in two groups. But UEFA's decision to have no semi-finals led to much cagey, uninspiring football.

England's tournament was disappointing. Serious crowd trouble marred a 1-1 draw with Belgium and they lost to a Marco Tardelli goal when they met hosts Italy. Despite beating Spain 2-1, when Trevor Brooking and Tony Woodcock scored, they were eliminated.

The Final, at least, was a spectacle and West Germany won when Horst Hrubesch scored the second of his two goals two minutes from the end to beat Belgium 2-1.

1980, Horst Hrubesch

1984: France, Winners: France

England paid for poor home form as they failed to reach the Finals for the third time in four tournaments, counting the cost of a goalless draw with Greece and a 1-0 defeat by a disputed penalty against Denmark, who went on to top their group.

Despite the absence of World champions Italy, who failed to qualify, the Finals in France ended with the hosts worthy winners, having played some of the most vibrant attacking football seen from a European team.

The re-introduction of semi-finals ensured that the sterile tactics of 1980 were not repeated. France's 3-2 win over Portugal, settled by Michel Platini's goal in the last minute of extra time, remains one of the finest matches in the history of the competition. France went on to beat Spain 2-0 in the Final, with Platini scoring his ninth goal of the tournament.

1984, Michel Platini

1988: West Germany, Winners: The Netherlands

For England and manager Bobby Robson, there was no repeat of the mistakes of the 1984 qualifying campaign. The only blemish came in a 0-0 draw in Istanbul against a Turkish team who would lose 8-0 at Wembley only six months later

Yet the Finals were a disaster. Beaten 1-0 by Jack Charlton's Republic of Ireland, they were blown away by a Marco van Basten hat-trick in a 3-1 defeat against the Netherlands and lost by the same scoreline to the Soviet Union.

The Soviets beat the Dutch 1-0 at the group stage but when they met again in the Final it was the Dutch who prevailed in a match memorable for the blistering, angled right-foot volley scored by Van Basten that clinched a 2-0 victory. It gave the Netherlands and visionary coach Rinus Michels their first international tournament success.

1992: Sweden, Winners: Denmark

Graham Taylor succeeded Bobby Robson and the 1992 qualifiers began with a relatively comfortable 2-0 win over Poland at Wembley but the rest of England's campaign was anything but straightforward. England drew away and at home to the Republic of Ireland but two unconvincing 1-0 wins over Turkey and a 1-1 draw against Poland in Poznan were enough to clinch a place in the Finals.

Yet England again flopped on the big stage, drawing 0-0 with Denmark and France and seeing David Platt's early goal overturned in a 2-1 defeat to Sweden.

Denmark, who were taking part in the finals only because of the withdrawal of war-torn Yugoslavia, then stunned the world by eliminating a strong Dutch side on penalties in the semi-finals and beating World champions Germany 2-0 in the Final, with Manchester United goalkeeper Peter Schmeichel one of their heroes.

1996: England, Winners: Germany

The Championship expanded to a 16-team 31-match final tournament, branded as 'Euro 96'. England, the hosts, made their best-ever showing, playing some glorious football under new coach Terry Venables.

After a 1-1 draw with Switzerland, England gathered pace with a 2-0 win over Scotland featuring a brilliant flick-and-volley goal by Paul Gascoigne, and then beat the Netherlands 4-1 in what remains perhaps their finest display in tournament football.

They won their quarter-final against Spain on penalties after a slightly fortunate 0-0 draw, but the ghosts of Italia 90 came back to haunt them after they ran into the Germans again in a gripping semi-final.

UEFA had introduced a 'golden goal' rule in the hope that matches might be settled without the dreaded shoot-out but, locked at 1-1 after 90 minutes after Stefan Kuntz had levelled Alan Shearer's goal for England, neither side could force the issue. So it came down to penalties again. As a nation held its breath, the first 10 went in. But Gareth Southgate's effort was saved.

The Final pitted Germany against the Czech Republic, who had been runners-up in their group and beat France, also on penalties, to reach the final. Again the 90 minutes ended with the scores level at 1-1 but this time there was a golden goal and Germany scored it, five minutes into the extra half-hour, through Oliver Bierhoff.

2000, France

2000: Belgium and the Netherlands, Winners: France

England finished a distant second to Sweden in their qualifying group but scraped into a new play-off round after Poland lost to Sweden in Stockholm. They booked a place in the Finals by beating Scotland 2-1 over two legs.

Kevin Keegan's side failed to progress beyond the group stage in the Finals, losing 3-2 to both Portugal and Romania each time having been in front. A 1-0 win over Germany proved to be a hollow revenge.

Portugal reached the semi-finals but lost by an extra-time penalty to France, who met Italy -- winners on penalties over the Netherlands in their semi-final -- in the Final in Rotterdam. There, Sylvain Wiltord equalised for the French in the fourth minute of stoppage time before David Trezeguet's 103rd-minute golden goal left the Italians shell-shocked.

2004: Portugal, Winners: Greece

Under Sven-Goran Eriksson, England were unbeaten in qualifying, with what proved to be the decisive match coming at the Stadium of Light in Sunderland -- Wembley was being redeveloped -- where goals from Darius Vassell and David Beckham beat eventual runners-up Turkey 2-0.

In the Finals, England lost to France but beat Switzerland and Croatia to reach the last eight, only to suffer another penalty shoot-out failure against Portugal, after injury had robbed them of star man Wayne Rooney early in the match. Ironically, Beckham and Vassell both missed their penalties.

Portugal beat the Netherlands to reach the Final in Lisbon only to lose to Greece, who had begun the tournament as 150-1 outsiders but proved that their 2-1 win over the hosts in the tournament curtain-raiser was no fluke. Striker Angelos Charisteas scored the only goal.

2004, Greece

2004, Wayne Rooney

2008: Austria and Switzerland, Winners: Spain.

UEFA scrapped the play-off round in favour of seven qualifying groups in which each team would play 12 times, the top two joining the hosts in the Finals. England stuttered with draws against Macedonia at home and Israel away and a defeat in Croatia.

Steve McClaren's team recovered well and in spite of losing to Russia in Moscow were second with one game left. However, defeat at home to Croatia combined with Russia's narrow win in Andorra sent Russia through as runners-up.

The tournament was won by Spain, who had a 100 per cent group record with victories over Russia, Sweden and Greece, then eliminated Italy on penalties after a goalless quarter-final, emphatically beat Russia again in the semi-final and shaded Germany in the Final in Vienna, decided by a goal from Fernando Torres after 33 minutes.

2008, Spain

5

Defenders

Rio Ferdinand

Born 7 November, 1978

Having won almost every trophy possible in club football, 32- year-old Rio Ferdinand would like nothing more than to round off a distinguished playing career with a major international trophy, especially after missing the 2010 World Cup Finals through injury.

The Manchester United centre-back began his career at West Ham, where his pace and ability on the ball enticed Leeds United to spend £18million to sign him in 2000. By then he had already won his first senior England cap as a substitute for Gareth Southgate in a friendly against Cameroon at Wembley, which at the time made him England's youngest-ever defender aged 19 years and eight days.

At Elland Road he helped the Yorkshire club to the Champions League semi-finals before making a £30 million move to Old Trafford in 2002 and blossoming into one of the best defenders in the world.

The South Londoner, who has won five Premier League titles, two League Cups and a Champions League title with Manchester United, has also been a mainstay of England's defence for the last decade. He won his 75th cap in Ukraine in October 2009, making him one of the 25 most capped England players in history.

DID YOU KNOW?

In 2009, Rio set up the 'Rio Ferdinand Live the Dream Foundation' which aims to help youngsters from deprived areas seeking careers in sport or entertainment.

John Terry

John Terry

Born 7 December, 1980

John Terry, who has captained England under both Steve McClaren and Fabio Capello, has been a focal point in the re-emergence of Chelsea as a trophy-winning club, and would love to have a similar affect on the national team.

Having spent his entire senior career at Stamford Bridge, Terry has become Chelsea's most successful captain of all time, winning three Premier League titles, three FA Cups and a brace of League Cups.

One notable goal the London-born centre-back has yet to fulfil is to win the Champions League, having gone agonisingly close in recent years, never closer than when he missed the penalty that would have won the tournament for Chelsea against Manchester United in 2008.

A constant threat in the air, Terry's consistency and commanding presence have seen him compete in three major tournaments with England since making his debut in 2003. In March 2009, he won his 50th cap.

His name will have a permanent association with the new Wembley Stadium. He scored the first full international goal there, for England against Brazil in 2007, and was the first FA Cup-winning captain there, for Chelsea against Manchester United in the same year.

DID YOU KNOW?

Chelsea accepted a £750,000 offer from Huddersfield Town for then 19-year-old John in April 2000 but he did not want to leave London.

Ashley Cole

Glen **Johnson**

Born 23 August, 1984

The first signing of the Roman Abramovich era at Chelsea, right-back Glen Johnson was part of the squad that won the Premier League title and the League Cup in 2005 before moving to Portsmouth, where improved performances earned him a move to Liverpool in 2009, after which his form enabled him to become an England regular.

Londoner Johnson began his career at West Ham but moved from East to West London when the Hammers were relegated to the Championship in 2003. Possessing fine pace and an eye for a telling pass, Johnson joined Portsmouth on loan in 2006 before signing a permanent deal for the 2007-08 season, helping Pompey win The FA Cup and earn European football for the first time in their history.

Liverpool paid £18 million to take Johnson to Anfield, where Kenny Dalglish identified him as a key component of his rebuilding job, with the Scot opting to use the 27-year-old as left-back towards the end of the 2010-11 season.

Having made his first appearance for the national team in 2003, Johnson has been an England regular only during the period of Fabio Capello's management, but some impressive displays in the 2010 World Cup qualifying campaign cemented his position as England's first-choice right-back.

DID YOU KNOW?

In 2007, Glen joined forces with former West Ham player Sam Taylor to set up the 'Glen Johnson Soccer School' in Dartford, Kent, to help train and develop local schoolchildren.

Ashley **Cole**

Born 20 December, 1980

Frequently described as the best left-back in world football, Chelsea's Ashley Cole has been virtually an ever-present in the England side since his debut against Albania in 2001 and is England's most-capped full-back.

A highly intelligent and quick defender, Cole's produced outstanding performances for England at Euro 2004, where he was named in Uefa's 'Team of the Tournament', and at the 2006 World Cup, where the accomplished manner with which he contained Cristiano Ronaldo won huge praise.

Cole, who excelled for Arsenal for many years before a controversial move to Stamford Bridge in 2006, has enjoyed a highly decorated career. A member of the 2004 Arsenal 'Invincibles' team, he has won three Premier League titles, six FA Cups and a League Cup.

The most noticeable gap in his CV is undoubtedly a Champions League winners' medal although the Londoner has twice been a losing finalist, once with Arsenal against Barcelona in 2006, and once with Chelsea against Manchester United two years later.

Even having passed his 30th birthday, Cole maintains a high level of fitness. During the 2010-11 Premier League season he started all 38 games for Chelsea on the way to being named the club's 'Players' Player of the Year' for the second time.

DID YOU KNOW?

American singer Mariah Carey discovered when researching her family tree that she is related to Ashley through a line from her grandmother in Alabama.

Glen Johnson

Michael Dawson

Born 18 November, 1983

Along with many other recent English centre-backs, Michael Dawson has found opportunities for the senior national team limited by the presence of Rio Ferdinand and John Terry.

But after some superb form for Tottenham Hotspur, helping them to secure a fourth place Premier League finish in 2010 to qualify for the Champions League, in which they reached the quarter-finals in 2011, he has been a regular feature in England squads.

Dawson began his career at Nottingham Forest, where at the age of just 18 he formed a strong partnership with veteran Des Walker to help Forest reach the First Division play-offs in 2003. After two-and-a-half impressive seasons at the City Ground, which led to him winning 13 England Under-21 caps, he moved to Tottenham in January 2005 and quickly became a favourite, scoring his first goal for the club against rivals Chelsea in 2006.

Tall and commanding, 6ft 2ins Dawson's tough tackling wins frequent praise, but his composure on the ball is similarly impressive and he is able to arrow the ball to the wings with consistent precision.
His height makes him a constant threat from set pieces so he provides a useful attacking option.

DID YOU KNOW?

Michael is the third member of his family to play professional football following older brothers Kevin (Nottingham Forest, Chesterfield) and Andy (Hull City).

Stephen Warnock

Born 12 December, 1981

A graduate of the famous Liverpool Academy, Stephen Warnock had loan spells at both Bradford City and Coventry City before making his Liverpool debut in 2004 against Grazer AK in the third qualifying round of the UEFA Champions League. His first (and only) goal for the Anfield side was during a 5-1 win against Fulham in March, 2006.

In January 2007, the left back joined Blackburn Rovers and made an impressive debut in the FA Cup fourth round 4-0 victory over Luton Town. The following month, he scored when Blackburn defeated Portsmouth 3-0. In August 2009, Warnock then moved to Aston Villa after agreeing a four-year deal with the Midlands club and, indeed, it was against his former employers Blackburn Rovers that he claimed his first Villa goal at the penultimate stage of the Carling Cup tournament on route to face Manchester United at Wembley in the Final of the competition.

Called in to the senior England squad for the first time in August 2005, the player was subsequently one of the 23 players chosen by coach Fabio Capello for the Finals of the 2010 FIFA World Cup tournament in South Africa.

DID YOU KNOW?

Did you know that TV impressionist Jon Culshaw was also born in Ormskirk, the birthplace of Stephen Warnock?

Leighton Baines

Born 11 December, 1984

Left-back Leighton Baines has become one of Everton's most consistent performers since moving from Wigan in 2007, and these displays have earned the Liverpudlian recognition on the international stage.

As a teenager, Baines was a key component of the Wigan side which rapidly rose from the lower leagues to the top flight, winning the Second Division (now League One) title in his first full season.

An intelligent passer, Baines confessed that he had doubts about his ability as a young player, originally fearful he would struggle to cope with the Premier League after helping Wigan to promotion from the Championship in 2005.

Those fears haunt him less now. The 26 year-old helped Wigan to the 2006 Carling Cup Final, before securing a £5 million move to Goodison Park. He had another taste of big-match atmosphere in the 2009 FA Cup Final and, after playing every minute of Everton's 2010-11 Premier League campaign, was named their 'Player of the Season'.

Capped 16 times at Under-21 level, he made his debut for the senior England side in March 2010 and has firmly established himself as prime understudy to Ashley Cole.

Phil Jagielka

Born 17 August, 1982

Everton's 2009 'Player of the Season', Phil Jagielka has stepped in successfully when Rio Ferdinand and John Terry have been missing through injury to establish himself as a key member of the England squad.

The Manchester-born centre-half began his career at Sheffield United playing in central midfield, where his dominant performances and some spectacular goals helped the Blades to promotion to the Premier League in 2006.

Jagielka has an exceptional ability to read a game, which made it no surprise that David Moyes spent £4million to secure his services at Goodison Park in 2007.

Since moving to Merseyside, the 28-year-old has concentrated his efforts on defensive work, although one of the highlights of his Everton career so far was scoring the winning penalty in the 2009 FA Cup Semi-Final against Manchester United, although a knee injury denied him an appearance in The Final.

After winning six Under-21 caps, he made his first senior England appearance in 2008 and his first start in the 4-0 win over Bulgaria in a European Championship qualifier in September 2010, when he was praised for his composed display.

DID YOU KNOW?

Phil is also a competent goalkeeper and kept a clean sheet when he took over from the injured Paddy Kenny for Sheffield United against Arsenal in 2006.

3 Defensive Greats

George Cohen

1964-67; Caps: 37; Goals: 0

Fulham defender Cohen was so highly regarded in football that the brilliant George Best once described him as "the best full-back I ever faced". He would have won more caps but for having Jimmy Armfield competing for the same position.

However, Armfield was injured during the build-up to the 1966 World Cup and Cohen took his chance to impress, so much so that by the time the Blackpool man was fit again he had lost his place as England's first-choice right back.

Cohen, whose overlapping runs made him ideally suited to Alf Ramsey's 'wingless wonders', was one of the unsung heroes of 1966, giving immaculate performances at the back and going forward.

George Cohen

Terry Butcher

1980-90; Caps: 77; Goals: 3

The iconic image of Butcher's bandaged head and blood-soaked shirt after he had refused to give way to a gaping head wound suffered in a vital World Cup qualifier against Sweden remains synonymous with defensive bravery.

But it was only one of many courageous performances by the former Ipswich and Glasgow Rangers centre-back, who played in three World Cups.

At the 1982, 1986 and 1990 tournaments, England lost only two matches out of 14 when Butcher was on the field and his absence from the 1988 European Championship was one of the key reasons for England's disappointing showing.

Terry Butcher

Sol Campbell

Sol Campbell

1996-2007; Caps: 73; Goals: 1

Sol Campbell was 21 when he gained his first senior England cap and two years later, in May 1998, became England's second-youngest captain, after Bobby Moore. He is the only player to have represented England in six consecutive major tournaments, playing in the 1996, 2000 and 2004 European Championships, and the 1998, 2002 and 2006 World Cups.

The youngest of 12 children from an east London family, Campbell found his expression in football and after starting out as a striker became an accomplished centre-half with Tottenham, Arsenal and Portsmouth. He won the Premier League title twice with Arsenal, where he was a member of the 'Invincibles' side that went through the whole 2003-04 season unbeaten.

Rivalries #1:

England v Germany

England's rivalry with Germany goes back to November 23, 1899, when a touring England team won 13-2 in Berlin, but the first official full international did not take place until 1930, again in Berlin, when a see-saw match ended 3-3.

England won the next seven games in a row, culminating in the 1966 World Cup Final, and it was not until two years later that the Germans won for the first time in a friendly.

Since then the tables have turned. England still have the edge in overall results -- 12 wins to Germany's 11 -- but have won only one of six more meetings in tournament finals and suffered four defeats, none more agonising than the penalty shoot-outs at Italia '90 and Euro '96.

It has led England to regard Germany as their biggest international rivals, yet the Germans themselves tend to be more excited when they face neighbours the Netherlands.

Gary Lineker, 1990 World Cup semi-final

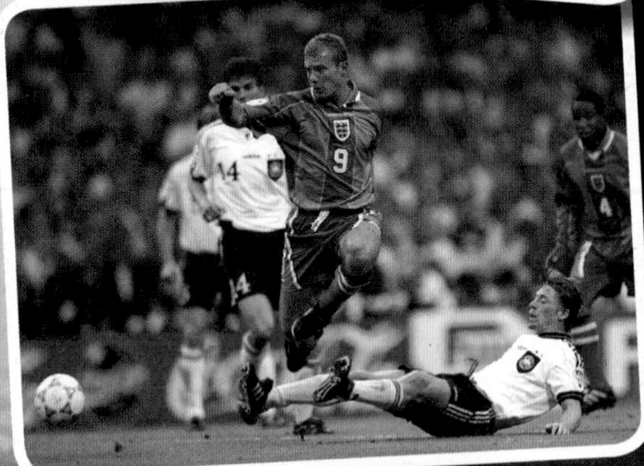

Alan Shearer, 1996 Euro semi-final

Geoff Hurst, 1966 World Cup final

England v Germany; the big matches:

Gerd Müller,
1970 World Cup quarter-final

1966: World Cup Final, Wembley
England 4, West Germany 2 (aet; 90mins: 2-2)
Hurst 3, Peters; Haller, Weber

1970: World Cup quarter-final, Leon, Mexico
England 2, West Germany 3 (aet; 90 mins: 2-2)
Mullery, Peters; Beckenbauer, Seeler, Müller

1972: European Championship qualifier, Wembley
England 1, West Germany 3
Lee; Hoeness, Netzer, Müller

1972: European Championship qualifier, West Berlin
West Germany 0, England 0

1982: World Cup second group stage, Madrid
England 0, West Germany 0

1990 -- World Cup semi-final, Turin
West Germany 1, England 1 (aet; 90 mins: 1-1)
Brehme; Lineker (W Germany win 4-3 on pens)

1996: Euro '96 semi-final, Wembley
England 1, Germany 1 (aet; 90 mins: 1-1)
Shearer; Kuntz (Germany win 6-5 on pens)

2000: Euro 2000 group stage, Charleroi
England 1, Germany 0
Shearer

2000: World Cup qualifier, Wembley
England 0, Germany 1
Hamann

2001: World Cup qualifier, Munich
Germany 1, England 5
Jancker; Owen 3, Gerrard, Heskey

2010: World Cup, Round of 16, Bloemfontein
Germany 4, England 1
Klose, Podolski, Müller 2; Upson

Michael Owen,
2000 World Cup qualifier

WEMBLEY factfile:

The new Wembley opened its doors in 2007 as home to the England national side, as well as host venue for the FA Cup Final and Semi-Finals, the Football League Cup Final, The FA Community Shield, the Football League Play-Off Finals and the Rugby League Challenge Cup Final.

The original Wembley Stadium -- demolished in 2003 -- was known as the Empire Stadium. It was built to be the centrepiece of the British Empire Exhibition of 1924.

With 90,000 seats, the new stadium has a capacity 10,000 fewer than the old one once had -- but there are no obstructed views and each seat has more leg room than there was in the Royal Box at the former Wembley!

Where the old Wembley was famous for its twin towers, the new version has its arch, visible right across London at 133 metres tall and, with a span of 315 metres, the longest single span roof structure in the world.

The stadium's pitch is a combination of synthetic grass and real grass, which strengthens the surface to enable the venue to host rugby, American football and music events as well as football.

Wembley in numbers...

107 -- the number of steps from the pitch to the Royal Box, compared with 39 at the old Wembley.

400 -- the total length in metres of the stadium's escalators.

600 -- the number of domestic television screens that would fit into each of the two giant replay screens.

688 -- the number of food and drink service points.

10,500 -- the number of seated meals that can be served at any one event.

30,000 -- the number of cups of coffee that can be dispensed automatically in just 10 minutes.

40,000 -- the number of pints of beer that could be served during the half-time interval.

98 -- the number of kitchens in the ground.

400 -- the number of seats in the press box.

2,618 -- the number of stadium toilets.

29 -- the number of seconds it took for Giampaolo Pazzini to score the first goal in the first professional match at the new Wembley on 24 March, 2007, as England Under-21s and Italy Under-21s drew 3-3.

npower
VAUXHALL

7

Midfielders

Steven Gerrard

Born 30 May, 1980

Steven Gerrard has been at the heart of England's midfield for more than a decade and shows no signs of stopping.

The Liverpool star made his England debut against Ukraine in May 2000, the day after his 20th birthday, and scored his first goal with a trademark long-range strike in England's famous 5-1 win over Germany in Munich the following year.

Gerrard missed the 2002 World Cup through injury, but has been involved at four major tournaments with England, including two quarter-final exits, both to Portugal, at Euro 2004 and the 2006 World Cup.

Aside from a Premier League title, the Liverpool captain has achieved almost everything in club football. Most notably, he inspired Liverpool to an astonishing Champions League victory in 2005, where they clawed back a 3-0 deficit against AC Milan in the Final in Istanbul before winning on penalties.

Dynamic and tough-tackling, the Merseyside-born player is usually employed in central midfield but his attacking instincts and goal threat have seen him play just behind a lone striker.

Frank Lampard

Frank Lampard

Born 20 June, 1978

One of the best midfielders of his generation, Frank Lampard has shone on the international stage ever since making his England debut in a friendly against Belgium in 1999.

The Romford-born player has appeared in three major tournaments, and was named in the Team of the Tournament at Euro 2004 after scoring three goals. His total senior appearances put him in the top 10 most-capped England players and the top five midfielders.

A constant goal threat, Lampard is a penalty specialist too. When he scored from the spot against Wales and Switzerland in 2010, taking his total to seven successful conversions, he overtook Ron Flowers and Alan Shearer to become England's leading scorer of penalties.

Lampard, another who has captained England, began his career at West Ham United, where his father, Frank Senior, was on the coaching staff, before moving across London in 2001 to Chelsea, where he has won three Premier League titles as well as appearing in three Champions League semi-finals and a Final, in 2008.

Steven Gerrard

DID YOU KNOW?

Frank scored England's 500th goal at Wembley against Slovakia in March 2009.

DID YOU KNOW?

Steven's home village of Whiston is also the birthplace of Melanie Chisholm, also known as Sporty Spice of the Spice Girls.

Stewart **Downing**

Born 22 July, 1984

Involved with the England side since his debut against the Netherlands in February 2005, Stewart Downing made a big-money move to Liverpool in 2011 that he hoped would further boost his prospects.

The 27-year-old began his career at Middlesbrough, where he helped the TeeSiders win the 2004 League Cup and reach the Final of the Uefa Cup two years later. He moved to Aston Villa after his home-town club was relegated in 2009, enjoying his best season with eight goals in 2010-11.

With a clever turn of pace, Downing can play on either wing but is naturally left sided and has enjoyed most of his success on that flank, possessing fine dribbling skills and crossing ability.

After winning seven Under-21 caps, Downing's attempt to establish a consistent place in the senior side was not helped by an injury suffered on tour with England but he has impressed enough to be selected by three England managers so far.

DID YOU KNOW?

Ashley played in the same school football team in Stevenage as world champion racing driver Lewis Hamilton.

Ashley Young

Stewart Downing

DID YOU KNOW?

Stewart's ambition before he made it in football was to become a top club DJ and has occasionally performed at clubs in Middlesbrough and Ibiza as an off-season hobby.

Ashley **Young**

Born 9 July, 1985

Ashley Young has joined Manchester United with huge expectations, but his form for England suggests he has the temperament to succeed at Old Trafford.

Having made his first start for the national side in August 2009 in a friendly against the Netherlands, the winger had to wait more than a year for his second full 90 minutes, in the Euro 2012 qualifier against Montenegro.

But he came off the bench to score his first England goal in a friendly against Denmark in February 2011 and scored again after coming on as substitute in the Euro 2012 qualifier against Switzerland in June.

Young's crossing ability and eye for goal first came to prominence as he helped Watford win promotion to the Premier League in 2006, with 5 goals in 41 league matches.

He joined Aston Villa in 2007, scoring on his debut, and rapidly established himself as a first-team regular, leading to his first appearance for England as a substitute against Austria in November 2007 after winning 10 caps at Under-21 level.

Gareth **Barry**

Born 23 February, 1981

England captain on one occasion, former left-back Gareth Barry is now a holding midfielder and the Manchester City man has been a lynchpin of Fabio Capello's squads.

Barry was a trainee at Brighton but moved from his Sussex birthplace to join Aston Villa in 1997, making his first appearance in the Premier League a year later, aged only 17.

At Villa, Barry established himself first as a composed defender and then the Birmingham club's key central midfielder. He won 27 Under-21 caps, equalling Jamie Carragher's record, and graduated to the senior England side as a substitute in a friendly against Ukraine in May 2000, making his first start in another friendly, against France, in September of the same year. Since 2007 he has been a regular.

Barry's impressive form with Villa saw him close to joining Liverpool in 2008. Just a year later, he moved to big-spending Manchester City, whom he has since helped win the 2011 FA Cup and qualify for the Champions League in the same year.

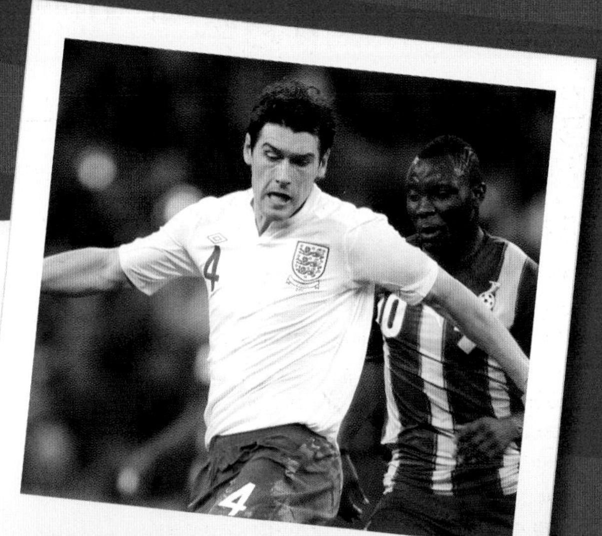

Gareth Barry

DID YOU KNOW?

Gareth and David Beckham are the only players to have been selected by every England manager since Kevin Keegan.

Aaron Lennon

Aaron **Lennon**

Born 16 April, 1987

Aaron Lennon's pace and dribbling skills make him a handful on the right of midfield, which has been one of England's most competitive positions and the Tottenham player has been a regular contender.

The stunning pace and quick feet that have defined Lennon's career were spotted at an early age, the Leeds-born player making his senior debut at 16 years and 129 days, at the time the youngest player to appear in the Premier League.

Lennon began his career with Leeds United but left after their relegation from the Premier League in 2005, with Tottenham securing his services for a bargain £1 million. He has flourished at White Hart Lane, winning the Carling Cup in 2008 and reaching the Champions League quarter-finals in 2011.

He earned his first England cap as a substitute in a friendly against Jamaica at Old Trafford in 2006 and made three substitute appearances in the World Cup in Germany that year. His first start came in a Euro 2008 qualifier in Israel in March 2007.

DID YOU KNOW?

Aaron became the youngest player ever to have a boot sponsor when he signed for Adidas in 2001, aged 14.

James Milner

Tom **Huddlestone**

Born 28 December, 1986

Tall, with a superb passing range and the ability to score spectacular goals, Tottenham's Tom Huddlestone has put himself firmly in contention for a spot in England's midfield.

Huddlestone was born in Nottingham but began his senior career at Derby County. The central midfielder made his debut for the Rams in 2003 when just 16 and spent two years in the East Midlands, helping the Pride Park side to the Championship play-offs in 2005.

He moved to Tottenham in the summer of that year. After a brief loan spell at Wolves, where he scored his first senior goal, he became a regular at White Hart Lane and captained the side in their famous 3-1 Champions League win over Inter Milan in 2010.

Huddlestone, who can also play as a centre-back, first represented England at Under-16 level, made 33 appearances for England's Under-21 team and made his senior debut against Brazil in 2009.

DID YOU KNOW?
Nottingham Forest had 6ft 3ins Tom on their books as a schoolboy but released him as a 12-year-old because they felt he was too small.

James **Milner**

Born 4 January, 1986

Manchester City's James Milner holds the record for the most appearances for England's Under-21 side with 46 and seeks to establish an equally regular place in the senior team.

Born in Leeds, Milner was a ball boy and season ticket holder at Leeds United's Elland Road ground before joining the club when just 10 in 1996. He made his debut at the age of only 16 in November 2002 and was the Premier League's youngest goalscorer when he found the net a month later.

Milner was sold to Newcastle in 2004 but had mixed fortunes on Tyneside and in 2008 joined Aston Villa, where he had spent a loan spell two years previously.

Under the guidance of Martin O'Neill, he blossomed into one of the Premier League's top midfielders. Adept on both wings of midfield and has also excelled in a central position. Capable of deceptive pace, his dynamic performances for Villa earned him his first England cap in 2009 and a place in the 2010 World Cup squad.

DID YOU KNOW?
James showed talent at cricket and long distance running before he concentrated on football and left school with 11 GCSEs.

Tom Huddlestone

Jordan **Henderson**

Born 17 June, 1990

There is no better indicator of the meteoric rise Jordan Henderson has experienced than the £16 million Liverpool were prepared to pay Sunderland for his services in the summer of 2011, little more than 18 months after breaking into the Wearsiders' first team.

The Sunderland-born player had a period on loan at Coventry City in the 2008-09 season and flourished under the guidance of Steve Bruce at the Stadium of Light, winning the club's Young Player of the Year award two years running in 2010 and 2011 for his composed, mature performances in central midfield.

Henderson played for England's Under-19, Under-21 and senior teams in the space of just two years. Despite playing 40 games in the 2010-11 club season, he also starred in the European Under-21 Championship in 2011.

Henderson, who initially played on the right side of midfield at Sunderland, capped an incredible period by making his England debut as a starter against France in November 2010, and the move to Anfield can only improve his prospects.

Scott Parker

DID YOU KNOW?

Scott appeared in a television ad for McDonald's as a 13-year-old, playing keepie-uppie as part of a 1994 World Cup promotion.

Scott **Parker**

Born 13 October, 1980

Combative midfielder Scott Parker had an outstanding 2010-11 Premier League season despite being relegated with West Ham and his form enabled him to revive his England career after a five-year absence.

Parker has played for England at every level from under-15 upwards and has won senior caps while with four different clubs.

He was with Charlton Athletic, where he made his first-team debut as a 16-year-old in 1997, when Sven-Goran Eriksson gave him his first appearance as a substitute against Denmark at Old Trafford in November 2003, had moved to Chelsea for £10 million by the time he won his second cap and was a Newcastle player when he made his first start, against Croatia in a European Championship qualifier in Zagreb in 2006.

His time at Chelsea was frustrating for Parker because of injury and limited chances in a star-studded squad but has been back to his best since returning to London in 2007. Named in Fabio Capello's provisional squad for the 2010 World Cup Finals, he did not make the final cut but has since won three more caps.

Jordan Henderson

DID YOU KNOW?

Jordan appeared on Soccer AM's Skills School in 2009 but was beaten by teammate Nathan Luscombe.

Michael **Carrick**

Born 28 July, 1981

Born in Wallsend in Tyne and Wear, Michael Carrick began his career at West Ham, making over 130 appearances before leaving for Tottenham in 2004 after the Hammers failed to win promotion from the First Division.

His career at White Hart Lane took off during the 2005-06 season, in which a string of influential midfield performances helped Spurs finish fifth, narrowly missing out on Champions League qualification.

The following summer brought a move to Manchester United, since when Carrick has won four Premier League titles as well as the Champions League and League Cup.

Carrick was capped 14 times at Under-21 level but senior opportunities have been fleeting since he made his debut in a friendly against Mexico in May 2001, although the midfielder looks set to remain an integral squad member for the foreseeable future.

DID YOU KNOW?
Michael scored twice as West Ham beat Coventry City by a record 9-0 margin in the two-leg FA Youth Cup final in 1999.

Michael Carrick

Jack Wilshire

Jack **Wilshere**

Born 1 January, 1992

Having performed with a maturity beyond his years in his career so far, Jack Wilshere represents the future of England's midfield.

The young Arsenal star has risen to prominence in the last three years, impressing first in Arsène Wenger's youthful League Cup teams and latterly in the Gunners' Premier League squad.

For Hertfordshire-born Wilshere, 2010-11 was a breakthrough season. Having spent the early months of 2010 on loan at Bolton, he made his first Premier League start for Arsenal in August and soon grew in stature, attracting particular praise for his assured performance in the 2-1 Champions League win over Barcelona.

Wilshere is the complete midfield package, a tough tackler and clever dribbler who possesses superb passing range. He made his Premier League debut in September 2008 at 16 years 256 days, a club record.

He first played international football as a 14-year-old in 2006, when he represented the England Under-16 team, and went on to play at all levels before making his Under-21 debut when he was still only 17. His first appearance for the England senior side came in August 2010 and he made his first start against Denmark in February 2011.

DID YOU KNOW?
Jack became only the fifth 16-year-old to appear in the Champions League when he played for Arsenal against Dynamo Kiev.

3 Midfield Greats

Alan Ball

Alan Ball was an industrious midfielder for Blackpool and went on to play for Everton, Arsenal and Southampton. At 21, he was the youngest member of England's World Cup winning squad in 1966. His energy and eye for a pass made him a major influence on England's success and his performance in the Final against West Germany was outstanding. Ball also appeared in the 1970 Finals.

He later went into management and proved more durable as a boss than most of his 1966 team-mates, taking charge of seven clubs, including Southampton, Manchester City and Portsmouth, whom he steered to promotion to the First Division in 1987. His death at the age of 61 robbed English football of a distinguished servant.

Alan Ball

Bobby Charlton

Charlton was almost the perfect attacking midfield player, an astute reader of a game with a natural instinct to go forward and one of the fiercest shots in the game. His part in the 1966 World Cup victory helped him become European Footballer of the Year.

The Manchester United man, a Munich air crash survivor, who had also played at the 1962 World Cup, scored England's first goal in the 1966 finals, against Mexico, and hit both goals in the semi-final against Portugal, widely seen as one of the national team's all-time finest performances. He appeared in his third World Cup in Mexico in 1970.

Sir Bobby, who managed Preston for two seasons after retiring as a player, has been a director at Old Trafford for more than 25 years.

Bobby Charlton

Paul Gascoigne

Paul Gascoigne

Gascoigne had skills that stood comparison with Diego Maradona but he was an unlucky player in many respects and not only at Italia '90, when he dominated the semi-final against Germany only to collect a caution that would have denied him a place in the Final, prompting tears shared by a nation. His career took more cruel twists through serious injury.

First, playing for Tottenham, he ruptured knee ligaments in the 1991 FA Cup Final, the damage keeping him out for more than a year. On recovery he completed a lucrative move to Lazio in Italy only for a broken leg in 1994 to cost him another entire season.

Even so, Gascoigne still won 57 England caps and in both the tournaments in which he played -- Italia '90 and Euro '96 -- he was the outstanding player.

The Netherlands 1, England 4

Wembley; 18 June, 1996; European Championship group match

Attendance: 76,798.

Goals: Shearer pen (23 mins) 0-1; Sheringham (51) 0-2; Shearer (57) 0-3; Sheringham (62) 0-4; Kluivert (78) 1-4.

A team encouraged to express themselves under coach Terry Venables deals the Dutch an unusually comprehensive defeat. England hit a purple patch early in the second half, producing football of exceptional quality.

The Dutch team is not a patch on the best to wear the orange strip and England are perhaps lucky to be in front through Alan Shearer's penalty at half-time after their opponents miss a number of chances.

But there is no dispute over England's second-half display, particularly in the first 17 minutes, when three goals put them 4-0 in front. The star of the show is Teddy Sheringham, who heads England's second, cleverly tees up the third for Shearer after a slick move involving Steve McManaman and Paul Gascoigne, then scores a second of his own.

Patrick Kluivert's goal is no more than token consolation for a team thoroughly beaten, while England celebrate to the strains of their Euro 96 anthem, 'Football's Coming Home.'

UMBRO

Rivalries #2:

England v Argentina

England's rivalry with Argentina developed from their controversial World Cup meetings in 1966 and 1986.

The first one, at Wembley, saw the Argentine captain, Antonio Rattin, sent off after arguing with the referee, then refuse to leave the field, holding the game up for 10 minutes.

The 1986 clash in Mexico is infamous, of course, for Diego Maradona's 'hand of God' goal, when the Argentine forward regarded by many as the most skilful footballer of all time appeared -- to everyone but the referee -- to use a hand to score the first of his two goals.

By then the rivalry had been stoked by the military conflict over the disputed Falkland Islands in 1982.

So far, overall, England have the edge in results, with six wins to Argentina's two, but one of the five draws -- in the 1998 World Cup -- had to be settled by a penalty shoot-out that Argentina won.

Diego Maradona, 1986 World Cup Quarter-final

Antonio Rattin, 1966 World Cup

England v Argentina: the big matches:

1962: World Cup group stage, Rancagua, Chile
England 3 Argentina 1
Flowers pen, Charlton, Greaves; Sanfilippo

1966: World Cup quarter-final, Wembley
England 1 Argentina 0
Hurst

1986: World Cup quarter-final, Mexico City
Argentina 2 England 1
Maradona 2; Lineker

1998: World Cup, round of 16, Saint-Etienne, France
Argentina 2 England 2 (aet; 90 mins: 2-2)
Shearer pen, Owen; Batistuta pen, Zanetti
(Argentina win 4-3 on pens)

2002: World Cup group stage, Sapporo, Japan
Argentina 0 England 1
Beckham pen

Michael Owen, 1998 World Cup

David Beckham, 2002 World Cup Group Stage

Darren Bent

Born 6 February, 1984

One of the most prolific English goalscorers in the Premier League, it is no surprise that Darren Bent is becoming increasingly recognised as a player with international quality.

The Londoner made his first impact for Ipswich Town in the Championship, having made his debut as a 17-year-old. He secured a move to Premier League Charlton Athletic in 2005 and enjoyed an impressive scoring record for Charlton before joining Tottenham in 2007 following the Addicks' relegation.

After a largely frustrating spell at White Hart Lane, Bent moved to Sunderland in 2009, where a season-and-a-half of prolific goalscoring persuaded Aston Villa to pay the Wearsiders a club record £24 million for his services in January 2011.

A player known for his positional awareness and cool finishing skills, Bent first played for England under Sven-Goran Eriksson against Uruguay in 2006, but has become a squad regular only recently. He scored his first international goal against Switzerland in September 2010, and followed it up with two in his next two matches against Denmark and Wales.

Wayne Rooney

Wayne Rooney

Born 24 October, 1985

One of the best players in world football, Manchester United's Wayne Rooney carries heavy expectations on his shoulders.

The Liverpudlian has won a host of club honours at Old Trafford, including four Premier League titles and a Champions League winners' medal. He had 50 England caps by the time he was 23 and has appeared in three major tournaments.

The dynamic forward began his career in his home city, at Everton, making his senior debut in 2002. When he struck his first goal, against Arsenal, five days short of his 17th birthday, he became at the time the youngest scorer in the history of the Premier League.

Carefully managed by David Moyes at Goodison Park, Rooney moved to Old Trafford in 2004, Sir Alex Ferguson spending £25.6 million on the 18-year-old. He has excelled for United, most notably scoring 34 goals in 44 games for United during the 2009-10 season.

Rooney rose to stardom so fast he skipped England's Under- 21s, making his senior debut aged 17 years and 111 days against Australia in February 2003, making him, at that time, England's youngest-ever player.

Darren Bent

DID YOU KNOW?

Wayne scored a hat-trick on his Manchester United debut in a 6-2 win over Fenerbahce in the Champions League.

DID YOU KNOW?

Darren, once a promising junior athlete who represented English Schools at long jump, has been clocked at 10.5 seconds over 100m.

Jermain **Defoe**

Born 7 October, 1982

A deadly finisher in the Premier League, Jermain Defoe has become a consistent England goalscorer.

The pacey Spurs man first displayed his natural poacher instincts at West Ham, close to his east London birthplace, but left Upton Park in 2004 following the club's relegation from the Premier League.

Defoe, who has over 150 senior goals, at first shone under Spurs manager Martin Jol but fell out of favour and linked up again with ex-West Ham boss Harry Redknapp at Portsmouth, following Redknapp back to Tottenham soon afterwards.

After seven goals in 23 appearances for the Under-21s, Defoe made his senior debut in 2004 against Sweden, and started for the first time later that year in a vital World Cup qualifier in Poland, in which he scored the winning goal.

Defoe has been to two World Cups with England, and scored the goal against Slovenia that took England into the last 16 at the 2010 Finals. The same year, he scored a hat-trick in a Euro 2012 qualifier against Bulgaria at Wembley.

Jermain Defoe

On loan to Second Division club Bournemouth as a West Ham teenager, Jermain equalled a post-war record held by John Aldridge by scoring in 10 consecutive League games.

DID YOU KNOW?

Peter was born in Macclesfield, Cheshire but his parents moved to Ealing before he was a year old and then spent a period in Singapore before settling in London.

Peter Crouch

Peter **Crouch**

Born 30 January, 1981

The tallest man ever to play for England, 6ft 7in Peter Crouch has established a remarkable strike rate in international appearances, scoring more than 20 goals at roughly one every two games.

Such a record seemed unlikely in the early stages of Crouch's career, which he spent in the Championship at Queen's Park Rangers and Portsmouth after he was released by Tottenham as a youngster.

Aston Villa signed Crouch in 2002. He failed to establish himself as a Villa Park regular but stayed in the Premier League with a move to Southampton two years later, where a sparkling year in 2005 saw him join Liverpool for £7 million, and make his senior international debut against Colombia in the May.

An obvious threat in the air but skilful with his feet as well, Crouch moved from Liverpool to Portsmouth in 2008, and was signed again by Harry Redknapp a year later when he returned to Tottenham, helping the side reach the Champions League for the first time in 2010.

Bobby Zamora

Theo **Walcott**

Born 16 March, 1989

Renowned for his blistering pace – Barcelona manager Pep Guardiola famously commented that it would require a pistol to stop him - Arsenal star Theo Walcott has represented his country at U16, U17, U19, U21 in addition to senior level.

As a teenager, the player arrived at Arsenal from Southampton in January 2006 and signed a professional contract on his 17th birthday two months later. He made his Premier League debut on the first day of the 2006/07 campaign against Aston Villa and provided the pass for Gilberto Silva to score in the 1-1 draw at the Emirates. His first Arsenal goal was against Chelsea in the 2007 League Cup final at the Millennium Stadium and by the end of Season 2008/09, he was fully established as a first team regular in Arsène Wenger's side. Although his 2009/10 campaign was marred by injuries, the forward ended the following season with a career high of 13 goals in all competitions.

During his first game for the England U-21 side, Walcott scored the opener against Moldova in the 2-2 draw at Ipswich's Portman Road ground. Two years later in 2008 at senior level away to Croatia in a qualifying game for the 2010 FIFA World Cup, he became the youngest player in history to score a hat-trick for England following the memorable 4-1 victory in Zagreb.

Theo Walcott

DID YOU KNOW?

Did you know that Theo's sister Hollie came second in the British Natural Bodybuilding Federation Central Championships in 2010?

Bobby **Zamora**

Born 16 January, 1981

Despite having his 2010-11 season seriously disrupted by injury, Bobby Zamora recovered his form at Fulham to catch Fabio Capello's eye and made his England debut against Hungary at Wembley in August 2010.

The 6ft 1ins Barking-born striker began his career at Bristol Rovers, but moved to Brighton in 2000, where he scored a remarkable 83 goals for the Sussex club in just three seasons, helping the Seagulls to successive promotions.

Zamora's goalscoring prowess brought a move to Tottenham in 2003, but he spent just six months at White Hart Lane before moving to the Championship with West Ham. He rediscovered his shooting boots there, helping the Hammers earn promotion to the Premier League and reach an FA Cup Final, before moving across the capital to Fulham in 2008.

After a barren first season at Craven Cottage, Zamora thrived under manager Roy Hodgson, with his goals integral to the club reaching the 2010 Europa League Final. Unfortunately, a broken leg halted his progress, forcing him to miss five months of the 2010-11 season.

DID YOU KNOW?

Bobby used to play in the same Sunday football team in east London as John Terry, Ledley King and Paul Konchesky.

Carlton Cole

Born 12 October, 1983

Powerful striker Carlton Cole will be hoping that West Ham's relegation from the Premier League does not interrupt his progress in international football after working hard to break into the England team.

The Croydon-born forward endured a frustrating start to his professional career after making his debut for Chelsea at the age of 18. Opportunities were limited at Stamford Bridge and, apart from loan spells at Wolves, Charlton and Aston Villa, he made only 32 appearances in five years in West London.

Cole did enjoy regular game time for the Under-21s over this period, making 19 appearances and scoring six goals. In 2006 he moved to West Ham, where his club career took off. He became an automatic pick at Upton Park in 2008, his commanding presence up front enabling him to score over 10 goals in each of the following three seasons, and win his first senior call-up.

Cole made his debut for England against Spain in February 2009, and was a regular in the 2010 World Cup qualifying campaign.

DID YOU KNOW?

In 2009, Carlton and West End star Gareth Gates both posed for a calendar to promote male cancer charity Everyman

Andy Carroll

Born 6 January, 1989

Saddled with the tag of the most expensive British footballer in history, Liverpool's Andy Carroll is determined to live up to such billing, for club and country.

Born on Tyneside, Carroll's spectacular rise through the ranks at Newcastle United culminated in Liverpool spending a remarkable £35 million for his services in January 2011. He had made his senior England debut against France the previous November.

Tall and powerfully built, the striker looks like an old-fashioned centre-forward, with a bustling style and keen eye for goal. He first came to the fore at Newcastle in 2009 but could do little to prevent the club's relegation that year.

He was able to fire his home-town club back into the Premier League at the first attempt, though, scoring 19 goals in 2009-10, before making an impressive start to life back in the top division, including a hat-trick against Aston Villa.

A big threat in the air, Carroll scored his first England goal against Ghana in March 2011, and his first goals for Liverpool against Manchester City the following month.

DID YOU KNOW?

When Andy moved to Liverpool, he was able to keep the No 9 shirt number he had been given at Newcastle because Fernando Torres was sold to Chelsea the same day.

3 Forward Greats

Nat Lofthouse

1950-58; Caps 33; Goals 30

Lofthouse stood only 5ft 9ins yet had a powerful physique hardened by pushing tubs laden with coal at his local pit, where he worked during his early days at Bolton Wanderers, the club he stayed with for his whole career.

His strength and skill, coupled with a powerful shot in either foot, made him almost the perfect centre-forward. He had courage, too, and became known as 'the Lion of Vienna' after an heroic performance against Austria in 1952, when he ran almost from the halfway line to score the winning goal in a 3-2 England victory, evading all attempts by defenders to hack him down before clipping the ball into the net even as the goalkeeper clattered into him. He was carried off on a stretcher.

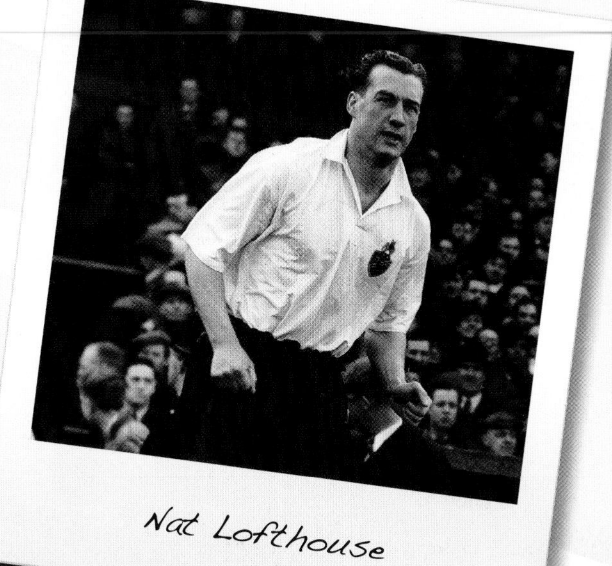

Nat Lofthouse

Jimmy Greaves

1959-67; Caps 57; Goals 44

The most prolific goalscorer in the history of top-flight football in England, Greaves had scored 100 League goals by the time he was 20 and reached 200 when he was 23, in a career that took him to Chelsea, AC Milan, Tottenham and West Ham. His career tally eventually passed 400 in all competitions.

He was no less effective in an England shirt, scoring a record six hat-tricks in a total of 44 goals bettered only by Bobby Charlton and Gary Lineker. Yet he missed out on England's finest hour in the 1966 World Cup, an injury early in the tournament letting in Geoff Hurst, who kept his place and famously scored a hat-trick in the Final.

Jimmy Greaves

Gary Lineker

Gary Lineker

1984-92; Caps 80; Goals 48.

Gary Lineker was a prolific goalscorer throughout his career, which saw him play for Barcelona in Spain and Grampus Eight in Japan as well as for Leicester, Everton and Tottenham in England.

As an international player, he was the key figure in helping England reach the quarter-finals of the 1986 World Cup in Mexico, when his six goals earned him the Golden Boot as the tournament's leading marksman. He also scored four times in the 1990 World Cup, including the goal that took England's semi-final with West Germany into extra time.

He retired after winning 80 caps, having fallen one short in his bid to match Bobby Charlton's record of 49 England goals.

ENGLAND TRIVIA:

01 When Cardiff City's Jay Bothroyd appeared as a substitute against France in 2010 he became the first player to represent England while playing club football in Wales.

02 More than 375 England goals have been scored by players from Tottenham and Manchester United.

03 Italy's 1-0 win at Wembley in 1997 ended England's record of never having lost a World Cup qualifier at home.

04 Striker Andy Cole's first four England appearances were for different managers -- Terry Venables, Glenn Hoddle, caretaker boss Howard Wilkinson and Kevin Keegan.

05 Sir Stanley Matthews, who was 19 when he scored his first England goal, was 41 when he scored his last, in October 1956.

06 England have played more matches in May than any other month.

07 When Newcastle striker Malcolm Macdonald scored all the goals in a 5-0 win against Cyprus in 1975 he became the first England player to score five in the same match since Tottenham's Willie Hall in 1938.

08 At 40 years and 293 days, Peter Shilton was the oldest player to captain England in the 20th century when he led the team out for the third-place match against Italy at Italia 90.

09 England were eliminated from the 1982 World Cup Finals even though they did not lose a game.

10 England have never lost more than three matches in a row.

11 Nottingham Forest midfielder Neil Webb became the 1000th player to be capped by England when he made his debut against West Germany in September, 1987.

12 Aston Villa have provided more England players than any other club.

13 England's World Cup-winning centre-half Jackie Charlton was on the losing side only twice in his 35 appearances.

14 The Liverpool winger Ian Callaghan, who made his England debut against France in the 1966 World Cup, had to wait 11 years and 59 days to win his second cap.

15 Bobby Zamora and Wes Brown are among 12 sets of cousins to play for England.

16 Graeme Le Saux and Matthew Le Tissier are the only players from the Channel Islands to represent England.

17 Steve Bull of Wolverhampton Wanderers is the last England player to be picked while his club was playing in the third tier of English football, in 1989.

18 The England team that finished the match against Switzerland in September 2010 contained six players from Manchester City.

19 Belgium, beaten 6-1 at Highbury in March 1923, were England's first Continental opponents on home soil.

20 Francis Jeffers, the Arsenal striker, scored for England on his debut when he appeared as a substitute against Australia in February 2003 but never won a second cap.

Quick Quiz Wordsearch:

Hidden in the grid below are the names of 17 England stars, past and present. See if you can find them all. Names can go across, up, down and diagonally.

N	O	S	B	O	R	R	L	P	R	L	T	J	M	K
N	E	V	I	L	L	E	F	P	R	J	E	Z	E	H
L	Q	N	F	R	L	C	H	V	B	L	Z	E	T	T
J	H	K	M	E	E	F	D	C	D	A	G	F	S	N
R	L	V	A	R	R	R	N	D	T	A	R	R	L	K
O	M	X	H	O	D	W	A	F	N	U	U	N	V	L
O	K	P	G	O	B	W	N	E	N	H	B	N	E	G
N	Q	W	N	M	A	N	I	P	H	L	R	N	A	S
E	N	B	I	N	N	Q	D	L	R	S	O	S	M	Y
Y	T	G	R	W	K	T	R	N	X	T	C	C	R	V
T	V	C	E	N	S	C	E	W	L	O	M	K	B	Y
W	E	H	H	M	H	M	F	R	I	L	L	L	X	J
X	F	R	S	L	N	X	A	G	H	C	U	O	R	C
Z	G	P	R	T	G	H	N	L	I	N	E	K	E	R
H	N	B	T	Y	C	E	N	G	C	C	Z	L	C	V

BANKS
BARNES
BUTCHER
CHARLTON
CROUCH
FERDINAND
GASCOIGNE
HURST
KEEGAN
LINEKER
MOORE
NEVILLE
ROBSON
ROONEY
SHEARER
SHERINGHAM
TERRY

Answers on Page 60

England Women

The England women's team showed the potential to become future world champions with their performances in 2011.

They reached their highest ever position in Fifa's world rankings after their quarter-final exit at the women's World Cup in Germany.

Kelly Smith

Although they lost to France in the last eight, their 2-0 group stage win over the eventual champions, Japan, helped them climb four places from 10th to sixth behind USA, Germany, Brazil, Japan and Sweden.

England had beaten both the Scandinavian side and the USA in friendlies before the World Cup, and their victory over Japan in the tournament itself reflected the huge progress made under manager Hope Powell.

Powell, who scored 35 goals in 66 appearances for England as a player, became the first full-time coach of the women's team in 1998. She has led the team to the quarter-finals of two World Cups and to the Final of the European Championship in 2009.

She is the first woman to be awarded the UEFA Pro Licence, having studied alongside England Under-21 Head Coach Stuart Pearce.

Under her guidance, players such as Rachel Yankey, Faye White and Kelly Smith have become well-known names. Smith and White, the England captain, play professional women's soccer in America.

Rachel Yankey

Faye White

Hope Powell

Germany 1, England 5

Olympic Stadium, Munich; 1 September, 2001; World Cup qualifier.

Attendance: 63,000.

Goals: Jancker (6 mins) 1-0; Owen (12) 1-1; Gerrard (45) 1-2; Owen (48) 1-3; Owen (66) 1-4; Heskey (74) 1-5.

Germany had lost only one home qualification match in their history and after winning 1-0 at Wembley the previous October did not expect to lose this one. They are a goal up after six minutes through Carsten Jancker.

But that is about the only thing to go wrong for England in their most impressive away win of all time. An inspired Michael Owen volleys a superb equaliser and Steven Gerrard rifles the ball home from 25 yards to put Sven-Goran Eriksson's team ahead at half-time.

Early in the second half, Owen makes it 3-1 and the Liverpool striker puts the game beyond doubt when he thrashes the ball past German 'keeper Oliver Kahn after Gerrard sends him clear. It is the first hat-trick by an England player against Germany since Geoff Hurst's treble in the 1966 World Cup Final. Emile Heskey outpaces the home defence to drill home England's fifth.

England Under-21s

Stuart **Pearce**

Head Coach, Under-21s

Throughout his career, Stuart Pearce has never taken anything for granted and never seen anything wrong with humility.

He became part of Nottingham Forest folklore, a figure revered by their fans; yet when he signed for the club in 1985, he felt it prudent to place an advertisement in the club's match programme, offering his services as an electrician, just in case things didn't work out.

Things did work out; he was a Forest player for 12 years, most of them as captain. His bulldog determination soon made him a huge favourite with Forest fans and his never-say-die attitude endeared him to England supporters, too, after he was called up for the first time in 1987.

He became known universally as 'Psycho' for his ferociously competitive spirit, although there were few players with a keener sense of fair play or who embraced the team ethic more wholeheartedly. If Gazza's tears made the enduring image of Italia '90, the picture of Pearce letting out a roar of relief after converting his penalty against Spain became similarly identified with Euro '96.

Pearce won the last of his 78 England caps in September 1999, aged 37, but remained a player until three days short of his 40th birthday, by which time he was wearing a Manchester City shirt. He remained at City as a coach and became manager in 2005, initially as caretaker, before being given the job on a permanent basis.

He joined the England coaching staff while still at City, taking up a full-time post as Under-21 Head Coach in July 2007.

Under his guidance, England reached the semi-finals of the 2007 UEFA Under-21 Championship, where they lost on penalties to hosts the Netherlands, and the Final of the same tournament two years later, losing to Germany.

England had a frustrating time in the 2011 tournament in Denmark, failing to qualify from a very tough group that included Spain, Ukraine and the Czech Republic.

Pearce's team drew with Spain and Ukraine but an improved performance against the Czechs was undone by two late goals, a 2-1 defeat enough to eliminate England.

3 Future Stars

Chris Smalling

Born 22 November, 1989

Greenwich-born Smalling progressed so quickly that little more than 18 months after joining Fulham from non-League Maidstone he had agreed terms with Manchester United.

A quick, intelligent central defender, Smalling's performances with Fulham soon earned him a call-up to England's Under-21s, for whom he made his debut in August 2009. A regular place in the senior side may not be far away.

Comfortable on the ball and, at 6ft 4ins, strong in the air, he did not need long to look at home in the centre of the United defence, revelling in the responsibility after an injury to Rio Ferdinand allowed him an extended run, making enough appearances to pick up a League winners' medal in his first season at Old Trafford.

Chris Smalling

Jack Rodwell

Born 11 March, 1991

Born in Southport, Rodwell played for Everton in Europe aged 16 years 284 days and made his Premier League debut against Sunderland two days short of his 17th birthday, making his first start in August of the same year and scoring his first senior goal in February 2009.

He captained England Under-16s when they won the Victory Shield in 2006 and made six appearances at Under-19 level before winning his first Under-21 cap against France at Nottingham Forest's City Ground in March 2009.

After helping England reach the Final of the European Under-21 Championship in 2009, when he scored in a 1-1 draw with Germany at the group stage, he became a firmly established member of Stuart Pearce's side.

Jack Rodwell

Daniel Sturridge

Daniel Sturridge

Born 1 September, 1989

Birmingham-born Sturridge scored four Premier League goals for Manchester City while still a teenager, earning a move to Chelsea in July 2009, and winning a first England Under-21 cap against the Netherlands the following month.

First-team openings for the 6ft 2ins striker have been limited at Stamford Bridge but Sturridge was given another chance to prove himself capable of making an impact against Premier League defences when he was loaned to Bolton Wanderers in January 2011.

He did not waste the opportunity, scoring the winner against Wolves on his debut and finishing the season with eight goals from 11 starts, returning to London determined to prove himself in Chelsea's colours.

QUIZ ANSWERS:

20 Questions, Page 14

1: Bryan Robson

2: Wayne Rooney

3: Theo Walcott

4: He was sent off -- the only player to be red-carded twice in an England shirt.

5: Gary Lineker -- six goals at the 1986 finals.

6: Tony Adams

7: Both failed to score in the penalty shoot-out that settled England's World Cup semi-final against West Germany.

8: All followed in their father's footsteps by playing for England.

9: Ryan Giggs

10: Graham Taylor

11: Steve Bruce

12: Peter Taylor, who was in charge for one game, a 1-0 defeat to Italy in Turin in November, 2000.

13: The controversial Derby, Leeds and Nottingham Forest manager, Brian Clough.

14: They are the only English-born England managers since Walter Winterbottom who did not represent the country as players.

15: Jermain Defoe

16: It made him the first black footballer to play for England.

17: The Fulham defender Zat Knight, who at 6ft 6ins is one inch smaller than Crouch.

18: They lost 1-0 to the United States in the World Cup in Brazil, at the time one of the biggest upsets in international football.

19: David Platt -- for Bari, Juventus and Sampdoria.

20: David Beckham -- for Real Madrid and LA Galaxy.

Wordsearch, Page 54

N	O	S	B	O	R	R	L	P	R	L	T	J	M	K
N	E	V	I	L	L	E	F	P	R	J	E	Z	E	H
L	Q	N	F	R	L	C	H	V	B	L	Z	E	T	T
J	H	K	M	E	E	F	D	C	D	A	G	F	S	N
R	L	V	A	R	R	R	N	D	T	A	R	R	L	K
O	M	X	H	O	D	W	A	F	N	U	U	N	V	L
O	K	P	G	O	B	W	N	E	N	H	B	N	E	G
N	Q	W	N	M	A	N	I	P	H	L	R	N	A	S
E	N	B	I	N	N	Q	D	L	R	S	O	S	M	Y
Y	T	G	R	W	K	T	R	N	X	T	C	C	R	V
T	V	C	E	N	S	C	E	W	L	O	M	K	B	Y
W	E	H	H	M	H	M	F	R	I	L	L	L	X	J
X	F	R	S	L	N	X	A	G	H	C	U	O	R	C
Z	G	P	R	T	G	H	N	L	I	N	E	K	E	R
H	N	B	T	Y	C	E	N	G	C	C	Z	L	C	V

BOBBY MOORE TRIBUTE

The honor of captaining England has been granted to 110 players since Cuthbert Ottaway led out the team to meet Scotland on November 30, 1872 for the first recorded international football match.

But only one has the distinction of being a World Cup-winning captain -- and 2012 brings a significant anniversary in the back-story of England's 1966 triumph. On 20 May it will be 50 years since Bobby Moore made his senior debut in the national colours.

It came during the build-up to the 1962 World Cup Finals in Chile as England played a friendly against Peru in Lima. They won 4-0 and Moore kept his place all the way through the tournament, ending with defeat by Brazil in the quarter-finals.

His selection did not meet with everyone's approval. Some newspaper pundits described the 21-year-old West Ham player as "pedestrian on the ground and suspect in the air". Four years later, after famously wiping his mud-stained hands on a velvet drape before shaking the hand of the Queen, he was lifting the Jules Rimet Trophy at Wembley.

Bobby Moore died in 1993, robbed of life by cancer at only 51, but 30 July, 1966 had immortalised him as a footballer. Four years after that, at the Mexico World Cup, came the ultimate in recognition, when he exchanged shirts with Pelé after an epic confrontation with Brazil.

Pelé later described Moore as "the greatest defender I ever played against" and said that Moore's England shirt was among his most treasured mementoes.

It was the greatest compliment any defender could be paid and justified every hour that Moore had spent on the training pitch as a young professional, determined to be the best player he could make himself. He never pretended to be the quickest defender and was certainly not the tallest. But through hard work he became a master of anticipation and timing, developing tackling skills that enabled him to take the ball cleanly off the feet of the most gifted forward and a jump that saw him seldom beaten in the air.

He won 108 senior England caps and was captain 90 times, a record he shares with another great defender, Billy Wright, having become England's youngest captain at the age of 22 against Czechoslovakia in May 1963.

Moore won an FA Cup and a European Cup Winners' Cup in his 642-game career with West Ham, although never the League title for which he felt their talented squad should have challenged.

He seemed to have the tactical acumen and experience to become a successful manager once he had finished playing yet attracted little interest from club chairmen. Eventually, he took a job as a co-commentator on a commercial radio station in London, just to remain involved in football. In fact, his last public appearance, a week before he died, was in the commentary position at Wembley for an England World Cup qualifier against San Marino.

ENGLAND